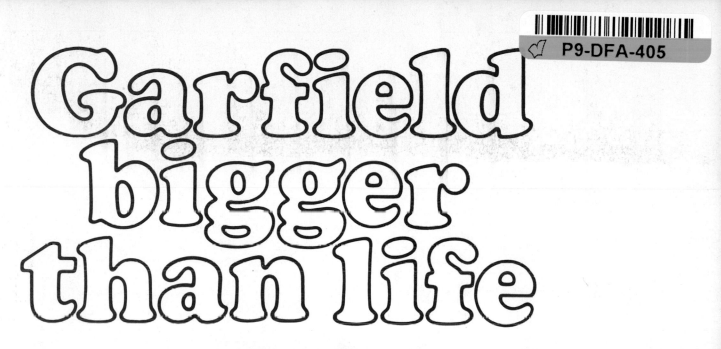

# Garfield bigger than life

BY: JIM DAVIS

BALLANTINE BOOKS · NEW YORK

Library of Congress Catalog Card Number: 81-066659

ISBN 0-345- 29796-2

Manufactured in the United States of America

First Ballantine Books Edition: November 1981

5     6     7     8     9     10

SPLOOSH!
OH-NO! A VICIOUS UNDERTOW IS DRAGGING ME OUT TO SEA!
I'M TOO YOUNG TO GO!
9-9
I CAN SEE THE HEADLINES NOW... "WORLD FAMOUS CAT LOST AT SEA. MILLIONS OF BEAUTIFUL GIRL CATS GRIEF-STRICKEN!"
I CAN'T MAKE IT! I'M GOING DOWN FOR THE THIRD TIME!
© 1979 United Feature Syndicate, Inc.
I'D SAVE YOU, GARFIELD. BUT I'M NOT ABOUT TO GIVE A CAT MOUTH-TO-MOUTH RESUSCITATION
JIM DAVIS

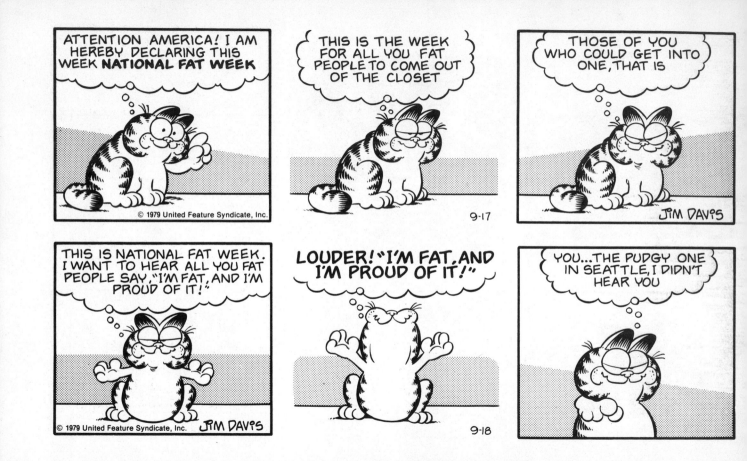

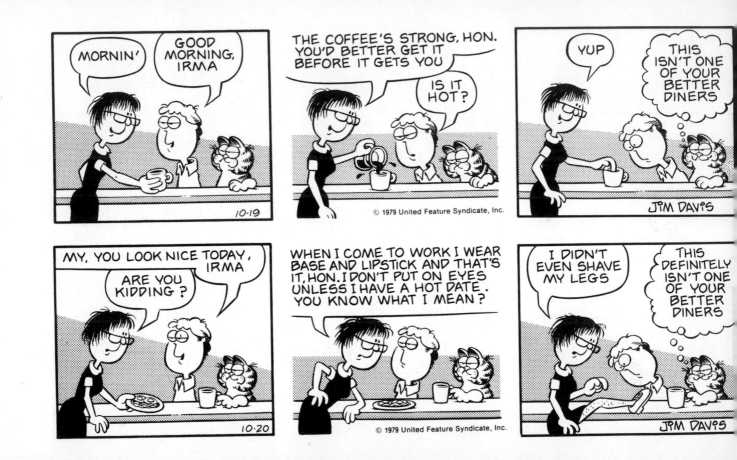

© 1979 United Feature Syndicate, Inc.

SMACK!

10·22

I HATE PATIO DOORS

JIM DAVIS

10-23    © 1979 United Feature Syndicate, Inc.

HEY, GARFIELD, WHERE'S ODIE?

HE'S EASY ENOUGH TO FIND

JIM DAVIS

JUST FOLLOW THE SLOBBER

© 1979 United Feature Syndicate, Inc.

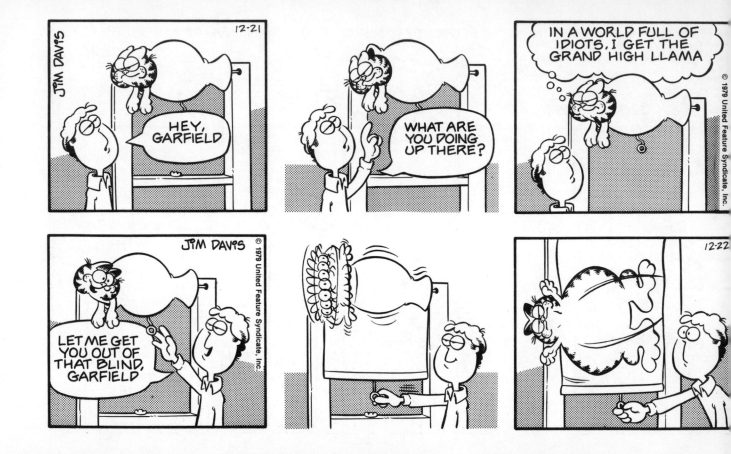

© 1980 United Feature Syndicate, Inc.

2-17

JIM DAVIS

© 1980 United Feature Syndicate, Inc.

GRACEFUL

BLOW IT OUT YOUR EAR

JIM DAVIS

# Garfield Up Close and Personal

**Q:** What is your favorite sport?
**A:** *Each morning, before breakfast, I like to take a good, brisk nap.*

**Q:** Where did you get your nasty temper, and why are you so cynical?
**A:** *Step a little closer and ask that.*

JIM DAVIS

**Q:** Describe your relationship with Jon, Odie, Pooky, and Nermal.
**A:** *Someone to abuse, someone to pound on, someone to confide in, and no comment.*

**Q:** Why did you call your most recent book "GARFIELD Bigger Than Life"?
**A:** *I didn't name the book, actually. I have the distinct feeling it is some kind of slur on my size. The book was named by my late editor.*

**Q:** How much money did you get for this book?
**A:** *Heavens to Betsy, I'm just a cat. That sort of thing doesn't concern me. Ask my agent.*

**Q:** Now that you are a success, do you give yourself your own baths?
**A:** *No, I've hired a cat to take baths for me.*

**Q:** Are you a prima donna?
**A:** *Not really.*

**Q:** Is there anyone with whom you would like to share the credit for your success?
**A:** *Not really.*